Precious Proof

True Stories to comfort and inspire

June Martin

Copyright © 2017 by June Martin. 722476

ISBN: Softcover 978-1-5434-8665-0
EBook 978-1-5434-8664-3

All rights reserved. No part of this book may be reproduced or transmitted in any form or by any means, electronic or mechanical, including photocopying, recording, or by any information storage and retrieval system, without permission in writing from the copyright owner.

The book is factual, only some of the names have been changed, to protect identities.

Print information available on the last page

Rev. date: 11/06/2017

To order additional copies of this book, contact:
Xlibris
0800-056-3182
www.xlibrispublishing.co.uk
Orders@ Xlibrispublishing.co.uk

This book is dedicated to my mum,
Joyce Cave (nee Wormald)
A lovely selfless and caring lady who was an inspiration and example to us all.
Miss you Mum x x x x x

Precious Proof

Introduction

It was about 15 years ago when I decided to write this book. The idea came to me whilst on a return journey from Scotland, with my boyfriend at the time. We were talking about family that had passed away and I could hear the emotion and sadness in his voice.

He had no belief in spirit or that loved ones lived on.

This was the point at which I realised how very fortunate I was to have had so many glimpses of spirit and so much evidence of the existence of another world. I'd had many magical experiences which were very varied in nature, and had been privileged to have shared heartfelt stories from my family and close friends. These insights have given me knowledge of this truth; that life does exist beyond death, and that there are many worlds beyond this one.

My wish is that by sharing these experiences, it may take away some of the pain that many feel when they lose a loved one. I know bereavement is different for everyone, and that grieving is a natural process.

I hope this book will bring a little comfort, peace, and hope to the reader, and to inspire people to look beyond the everyday world: for the unseen, which I believe is as wonderful and magical as the material world and is interwoven with it.

I have also included some of my favourite poems, sayings and insights from some of the wise people that have passed through this Earth and inspired many.

I would like the reader to know that I am no "pushover", not easily convinced of things, but logical and rational.

As a young girl in religious education lessons, though I believed in Jesus Christ I found it very difficult to believe in God. I did not understand suffering or why innocent people had to suffer. It is a question that has perplexed and puzzled many from ordinary folk to great philosophers. It is a question I still do not fully understand, but these experiences are my proof that life does exist beyond death.

I hope you enjoy this book.

~~~~~~~~~~~~~~~~~~~~~~~~~~~

"There is no sorrow like separation" - The Dharmapada sayings of Buddha.

Sleep Now My Angel

Sleep now my angel
And rest a while
Let pain and sorrow
Slip away
Like the caterpillar
Lying dormant
You too will awake
With new eyes
To a new world
That we can only
Try to imagine
Life is wonderful
And full of endless mysteries
Love and thought fly
Unbounded by flesh and bone
Fast, faster than light
Across the universe
When I think of you with love
You will know
And in time, the sorrow of our parting
Will be easier to bear

June Martin

The Embryo

My first real encounter with spirit was when I was Eighteen years old. I rented a small basement bedsit in a big Victorian building on the edge of Hyde Park in Leeds. The building was very long and three floors high. It was divided into bedsits and flats, but despite the amount of people living there it was very peaceful and quiet.

I was lying in bed fast asleep one night, when I was awakened by three very loud knocks. I shot around in my bed and stared towards the door. There stood two beautiful figures, shining as though they were made of light. The taller was white and the smaller pale blue, they were dressed in long gowns (they didn't have wings). Even though they were beautiful I was literally petrified, I couldn't move or speak, I just lie there, as stiff as a board and staring, until after what seemed like a few minutes they faded and disappeared. I laid motionless wondering why they had come, and wishing I could have spoken to them, and found out who they were and why they had come to visit me.

It was to be several years before I understood why they appeared that night.

To this day it is a chapter in my life that I am ashamed of.

It was the era of 'free love'. People drifted in and out of relationships most irresponsibly and I was no exception!

I had a brief relationship with a young man who was nicknamed 'Curly'. He was very well educated smart and clever and I was fascinated by him. I didn't have a lot of self-confidence at that young age and wondered why he wanted to go out with me. Sadly, coming into a lot of money at his young age had made him wary and mistrustful of his friends. He didn't treat me very nicely and even one of his own friends asked me why I put up with him.

We had been seeing each other a couple of months when I realised that I had missed a period and tested positive with a pregnancy testing kit. I was very immature myself, and had no idea what to do, so I turned to my family for guidance and advice, and decided that it would be best to have a termination.

I was young and naïve and didn't think of this tiny embryo as a baby.

Curly wanted me to have the baby (though I am sure he didn't love me). He even suggested that my Mum could bring the baby up. But when he asked me why I was having an abortion, the cruelest words I've ever said blurted out of my mouth. 'Because you're the father', I shouted. We had an altercation and he left through a ground floor window that was open. I never saw him again after that day.

The significance of this story will be clear by the end of this chapter!

Several years later, Mum went to a service at a Spiritualist church that she attended regularly. There was a weekly meeting in the upstairs rooms at the back of Woolworths in Leeds.

It was my birthday 7th June when Mum said that she had received a message at church. The message was of a beautiful girl in spirit with long blond wavy hair (as her father had) and she would be about seven years old. Mum said she knew it was my daughter, but at that point I wasn't convinced.

Again many years later I had some more significant proof when I went to see a lady called Betty, ('Little Betty' to her friends) who I knew quite well.

Betty had been very poorly so I went to see her at the local hospital and took her some flowers. However, when I reached the ward she had been discharged.

I went to her home and was pleased to find her feeling much better. We shared a cup of tea, and whilst I had heard that Betty was known to be a bit psychic, I never expected what followed.

She said 'there is a beautiful girl stood to the left of you. She has long blond wavy hair and is totally unblemished, as though she is not of this world'. 'She is showing me that her Dad slapped you across the face'.

I was both amazed, and fascinated. Now I really did believe my daughter was in spirit. Betty could not possibly have known what had happened all those years before as I had told no one about this.

I told the story of what had happened. 'Her name is Crystal' said Betty, ' She has moved to your right side now because you have accepted her' she said.

It was a wonderful thing to discover that I had a daughter called Crystal who had grown up in Heaven.

I believe the two figures I saw were Crystals surrogate parents in the spirit world and that they had loved her and cared for her.

The conclusions of this story are very far reaching. It means not only that little embryos live on in spirit, but somehow they are raised in Heaven.

Luke chapter23 verse43
And Jesus said unto him 'verily, I say unto thee, today thou shalt be with me in paradise'.

In my Father's house there are many mansions, if it were not so I would have told you, I go to prepare a place for you' – Jesus Christ

We are not able to see our life after death, just like we are not able to see our life before we are born, because we are not able to imagine anything beyond the time. - anon

Essa Mohamed Guye

I got married for the first time to Peter (my second husband is also called Peter) in March 1977. We found a flat to rent in Spencer Place, Chapeltown, Leeds. It was a notorious street, a 'red light' area, but I loved living there and we had really nice neighbours.

It was then that Peter introduced me to a man called Mr Guye, a tall slim African man who appeared to be very wise but also modest. He very soon became a friend.

Mr Guye was no ordinary man! His sitting room would regularly be full of people waiting to see him, usually for advice. He also read shells, small cowrie shells which he kept in a small drawstring bag. He would look to be in deep concentration as he shook the shells in his hands and dropped them on the floor, sometimes several times. He then would interpret what he had seen.

This was not his only means of 'seeing' however, and on more than one occasion I had walked into his living room and he had known exactly why I came before I even opened my mouth.

Mr Guye's full name was Essa Mohamed Guye, and he professed to be both a Muslim and a Christian. I felt lucky to have come to know such an interesting man. He would always make you welcome and had a massive pan of herb tea on the go, which he claimed was responsible for his good health. He usually wore a suit, but on occasion he would wear his traditional African clothes, and then he would appear to glow.

After some months of marriage, I discovered I was pregnant with our first child.

On one visit to his house I asked Mr Guye out of curiosity, 'what does the name Essa mean?' He said that it was Muslim for Jesus. Without a second thought I said ' if my child is born on Christmas day and he is a boy I will call him in your name'.

My baby was due on the 17th of December and I had no idea what sex the baby was. The due date came and went, and sure enough on Christmas morning 1977, I started having contractions, and I gave birth to a beautiful baby boy, born at 7.30pm on Christmas day at our home on Spencer Place, Chapeltown. Attended by my husband, two African midwives, and the two Grandmas, who were pacing around the living room anxiously!

I would have given him Essa as a first name, but my husband was reluctant saying he would be teased when he got older, so we agreed to make Essa his second name. I read names from the Bible that I liked, and when I said David he opened his eyes, and looked at me. So he was named David Essa.

He was indeed a mythical child as I was to discover when he was older.

Whilst I lived in Chapeltown we visited Mr Guye on many occasions, and I will never forget some of the wise things he taught me.

My favourite wise words from Mr Guye ' Be careful what words come from your mouth. Once they are out you can't put them back'

Mr Guye's recipe for Porridge, (Perfect every time!)
1 cup of porridge oats
1 cup of milk
1 cup of water
Bring to boil slowly, stir and simmer for 1 minute.

The conclusion of this story is that that some things are indeed predestined and also the future can be foretold. I am also sure our intuition is much underestimated, and a lot closer to the divine than our rational mind.

My Granny

It was the winter of January 1978 and David our first baby was less than 2 weeks old. We had snuggled him up in his pram and gone for a walk to the local park.

About half way round the park we met up with my Mum. When she had called and found we were not in she had followed the pram tracks in the snow and found us.

As we walked back towards the flat she said that she had come to tell us that my Gran had passed away.

This is as she told me: 'Your Aunt Betty rang me, and said that she knew that your Gran was dying and she couldn't cope' (Aunt Betty lived with my Gran and looked after her at their home in Raistrick, Near Brighouse). Mum immediately went over. Aunt Betty overcome with emotion, had left Mum to sit with my Gran. After some time, Gran let out a long sigh; her last breath.

As my Mum watched, the room filled with the most beautiful colours she had ever seen, and she watched as Grans face changed back to being young.

My Gran was 89 when she died; she was suffering badly from arthritis, so like many more it was a mercy. It was lovely that she was able to go peacefully and leave us with such comforting and special memories.

My only sadness was that she had not been well enough to see David before she died. He was her first great grandchild.

The consequence of this story is that in the spirit world, we return to our younger appearance. My Mum believes that you don't age past twenty-one in Heaven! Haven't we all wished we knew what we know in later life and still had a young body!

A Smile Costs Nothing

A smile costs nothing, but gives much. It enriches those who receive, without making poorer those who give, It takes but a moment, but the memory of it can last forever. A smile creates happiness in the home, brings cheer to the discouraged, sunshine to the sad, and is nature's best antidote to trouble. Yet it cannot be bought, begged, borrowed or stolen, for it is something that is of no value to anyone until it is given away. Some people are too tired to give you a smile, give them one of yours, as none needs a smile as much as he who has no more to give.

Anon

Beware of the dark side

Some years later we were living at Conway Grove in Harehills, when Pete (my first husband) told me a story of something that happened to him when he was a teenager.

Pete spent his childhood further up the same street in a terraced house with his Mum, Aunt and Uncle.

One time, in his late teens, he had a few of his friend's round in his attic bedroom and they decided to mess around with a Ouija board. They probably thought it was harmless, but the atmosphere changed. The attic door slammed and terrified, Pete's friends fled from the room. Pete saw a grotesque vision. On the wall appeared a face, a pigs head with horns. Pete was so scared, he could not get it out of his mind, and though he was not religious, he sunk to his knees and prayed for help.

Shortly afterwards he found a small cross with sparkling blue stones in the house. He showed the cross to his Mum his aunt and his uncle but they all said it was not theirs and they had never seen it before.

Once he wore the cross and he felt safe, the horrible vision no longer troubled him.

I believe there is a special magic in crosses, and have more experiences in this book connected with crosses. I also believe that The Lord's Prayer and the herb Rosemary have the power to dispel evil.

Confucius he says......................
For those who don't know Confucius was a sage, a wise man and a great philosopher. He was asked by one of his students what he regarded to be his highest teaching. He paused then said 'Do not let evil enter your thoughts' and equally ' The best way to combat evil is to work energetically for the good'

The Horse Race

Whilst living in the same house in Harehills I became aware of the dangers of Nuclear weapons and wanted to do something about it in my own small way. I joined the peace movement and started the Harehills Peace Group. We did a few showings of 'The War Game' a film about what life would be like in the event of nuclear war and gathered signatures for the world disarmament campaign. I was genuinely shocked and afraid what could happen, and the terrible consequences of nuclear war.

Our little peace group did not achieve much but we tried!

At that time Pete loved horse racing and regularly watched races on TV. I wasn't particularly interested myself, (in fact it irritated me!) but one day when he was watching the races, there was a lovely dapple grey horse running called No Bombs. I thought to myself: if this horse wins, the world will not end in a nuclear war.

Strange thought I know, and I did not take it that seriously. I was not even paying that much attention until near the finish line where No Bombs was in a big group leading the field.

They crossed the finish line and the commentator announced a photo finish. They could not discern which horse had won. It was the <u>first ever</u> photo finish between five horses. No bombs won by the tip of his nose. It gave me a shiver, it would not have meant so much had it not been such a close and rare thing, but I felt strangely reassured.

Knowing the capabilities of Nuclear weapons and their devastating effect, how close have we come to destroying this beautiful planet on which we all live and depend.

The Red Indian Ten Commandments

Remain close to the Great Spirit
Show great respect for your fellow human beings
Give assistance and kindness wherever needed
Be truthful and honest at all times
Do what you know to be right
Look after the wellbeing of mind and body
Treat the Earth and all that dwell thereon with respect
Take full responsibility for your actions
Dedicate a share of your efforts to the greater good
Work together for the benefit of all mankind

If only we all lived by these laws what a wonderful world it would be.
I would have loved to be a red Indian, they were so respectful of nature, it is a great shame they were pushed out of all their lands. We have such a lot to learn from them.

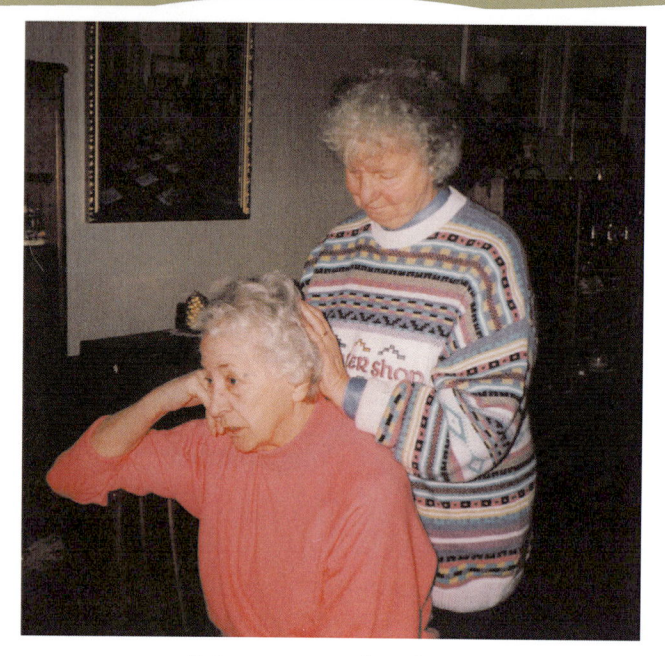

Mum giving healing

The Women's group

It was while we were living at Conway Grove in Harehills that my second boy Michael was born at home. I was a little nervous wondering how David would feel, from being the only child and now having a little brother.

I took David up to see his brother for the first time. He leant over the cot gently stroked his head and just said 'lovely'.

Michael was a real cutey with big bright blue eyes and wispy blond hair; I used to call him my little Buddha.

Several months later I joined a local women's group in Harehills which held weekly meetings at a local community centre.

We had decided to have some sessions on alternative medicine as a lot of our small group were interested in learning more.

The first talk we had was on acupuncture, and a lovely lady called Magda came to talk to us. The second was on homeopathy which fascinated me. This talk was given by Jo More who later became a friend. I bought a couple of little prescribing books from her, and later used them to help some friends and family.

The third talk was from my Mum and was about healing.

Mum had first become interested in healing after reading a book by the famous healer Harry Edwards, who was a truly good and genuine man.

Mum had hoped that healing could help my brother John who suffered from epilepsy. She took my brother to healing every week and sure enough he was clear of seizures by the time he was in his teens.

Sadly, John's epilepsy returned when he was in his twenties, triggered by an anaesthetic given to reset a broken ankle.

Going back to the talk, everyone listened intently, and then Mum offered to give healing to other members of the group. Whist Mum was giving healing the rest of us were talking, and as it turned out two other members of the group regularly had psychic experiences.

One lady whose name has escaped my memory said that she had received messages for people who were going through problems. A voice would tell her what to say and to whom. She would then ring or call to see the friend or relation and relay the advice, never revealing that she had been told by a spirit voice (this is called clairaudience as opposed to clairvoyance when a person sees spirit or clairsentience when a person senses spirit). We were all amazed.

Then, Juliet Pearce who led our group told us of her experiences. Juliet was a qualified physiotherapist and worked for the NHS for many years. She said that often she felt that she was not really doing the clients a great deal of good, but on some occasions, when she had felt great compassion for one of her clients, a surge of energy would come through her hands. It was very powerful and she was even a bit scared herself!

Without fail when this happened, the client would say to her afterwards that when she had put her hands in this place ' it was amazing'. We were only a small group of women, about eight in number, but what fascinating experiences came out in the open that day.

The conclusion of this story is that there is a very strong connection between compassion and healing, and also that there are many amongst us who have some kind of sixth sense or spiritual side that they talk very little about. I have found that the more you open up and talk about these experiences, the more you will realise that they are not uncommon, but all are unique.

"If you want others to be happy practice compassion. If you want to be happy practice compassion"- **The Dali Lama**

<u>Take time</u>

Take time to think; it is the source of power.

Take time to read; it is the foundation of wisdom.

Take time to play; it is the secret of staying young.

Take time to be charitable; it is the path to Heaven.

Take time to love and be loved; it is God's greatest gift.

Take time to laugh; it is the music of the soul.

Take time to be friendly; it is the road to happiness.

Take time to pray; it is the greatest power on earth.

Author: Unknown

I would like to include the following story, not so much for proof of the afterlife but because it is about Ghandi who is an inspiration, and proof that one person can make a fantastic difference to the world.

Ghandi

I remember when I was about 15. My sister Hazel and I went to the Odeon cinema in the centre of Leeds to see the film Ghandi. If you have not seen this film, I would highly recommend it.

Trained as a lawyer in England, Ghandi first tried to bring about change in South Africa where the evil system of apartheid was in full swing. Ghandi and his wife set up a small community. They were trying to bring about change by non-violent acts of civil disobedience.

In one scene Ghandi and his wife Indira had an argument; Indira had been raised in India's equivalent of upper class. Ghandi insisted on treating everyone as equals, so when his wife refused to take her turn cleaning the latrines, Ghandi was annoyed.

I remember her line when she gave in, and did as she had been asked. She said 'The trouble is, husband that we don't all want to be as good as you'

The evil of South Africa proved too much for even Ghandi to change. He and his followers suffered constant beatings by the South African police.

He returned to his native India, where he proceeded to overthrow the British imperial forces that had taken over. They were treating the natives like second class citizens.

He changed the world through simple words and actions and was totally against violence.

`He never desired riches or honours and would insist on serving tea to his colleagues. He would even break from a meeting to attend to a sick goat.

Eventually he became the ruler of his country.

At one point during Ghandi's rule, fighting broke out between different religious factions and some people were even killed. Ghandi was greatly saddened by this and responded by refusing to eat until the fighting stopped.

The trouble continued until the point that Ghandi was really weak and they feared he would die. When the word was spread about Gandhi's condition, all the fighting stopped and peace was restored. Such was the love and respect that people had for him.

What a man of courage, wisdom and sincerity. Like many great men, he was assassinated.

When the film finished the entire audience stood up for a standing ovation. It was really moving.

Gandhi always refused to say that he belonged to one religion. He said his preacher as a child taught from one religious book and then another, not making any difference.

We can all learn a lot from Mahatma Gandhi. If only all politicians were as wise then what a different world it would be.

Many people, especially ignorant people, want to punish you for speaking the truth, for being correct, for being you.

Never apologize for being correct, or for being years ahead of your time.

If you're right and you know it, speak your mind. Even if you're a minority of one, the truth is still the truth. ~Mahatma Ghandi

It is the action, not the fruit of the action that is important. You have to do the right thing. It may not be in your power, it may not be in your time that there'll be any fruit. But that doesn't mean you should stop doing the right thing. You may never know what results come from your action. But if you do nothing there will be no results.

~Mahatma Ghandi

The Mysterious Painting

My marriage to Pete only lasted 4 years. After we parted I stayed with a friend and eventually rented a house from housing co-operative in Vicars Terrace, Harehills, Leeds. It was a lovely house.

I was expecting my third baby when I moved in. I had lots of friends around me, including my friend Cathy's boyfriend Steve who was an artist.

One day I asked Steve if he would paint a picture for me for my new house. He agreed, and a few weeks later he returned with a really unusual painting. He said that he had never painted anything like it before and he had been inspired to paint it.

The painting was of a cave with a stream flowing from it. In the centre of the stream there was a Lotus flower, and at either side there were three Chinese figures in long white robes. One of the figures was carrying a sword, one a staff and one bare handed.

Steve said that the figures were my three sons, and that I was the mystery that was in the cave! It was a very mysterious and beautiful gift, and indeed my third child turned out to be another boy, Samuel Luke.

The conclusion of this story is that, there is a strong possibility that reincarnation is a reality. Many of us may have past lives. This may be flimsy evidence on which to base such a far reaching conclusion, but Steve was so genuine that I am sure what he told me was true. There are also many stories from adults and children who have remembered a previous life that have been found to be historically correct

My good friend Sue

A few months after I had moved in I had a brief relationship with Skinny, an old friend that I met up with (his real name was John). We were seeing each other for a while when one day he turned up with a lady called Sue.

Sue was a breath of fresh air. When she came into the house it was as though the countryside had entered our front room. Despite being a Yorkshire lass, Sue had a strong Scottish accent, which she had picked up over the years she had lived there. We became instant friends.

Sue had gone through the most terrible and unimaginable tragedy, a few months prior to her returning to Leeds.

Her only daughter Theresa, a bright, intelligent and popular girl had died under tragic circumstances, aged just sixteen. Theresa, or Terry as she was nicknamed, had gone to a party at a friend's house and someone had given her a Camden tablet instead of a paracetamol for a joke, not realising the harm it would cause. The Camden tablet burnt through her stomach, there was nothing the paramedics could do to save her. Sue watched helpless as she died in agony.

She couldn't face staying in Scotland so she had returned to Leeds.

Skinny had been her childhood sweetheart and he took Sue under his wing.

Sue was the person who introduced me to Herbal medicine.

When Sam was only a few weeks old, I got mastitis (caused by blocked milk ducts). My breasts were very sore and tender. Sue brewed up a massive pan of raspberry leaf tea, and sure enough within a couple of days I was completely better. After that I bought a Herbal book and started reading and consulted it regularly, using herbs to treat myself and my family.

One day Sue came to visit and gave me a lovely rosary for Sam. It had green glass beads and a crucifix.

I felt so honoured as it had belonged to her daughter Theresa. I took the rosary and wrapped it around the post on Sam's cot.

A couple of weeks later, I went to pick Sam up out of his cot, and noticed that the cross had gone from the end of the beads.

I searched the cot and then the room and couldn't find it anywhere. I looked high and low all over the house, but still no cross. I couldn't bear to tell Sue that it was lost, it had been so lovingly given and so special, having belonged to her daughter.

One evening about a week later, Skinny and Sue came to the door. She stood on the hallway, and opening her hand she said 'Is this Terry's cross'. I felt my face turning fifty shades of scarlet! I was so embarrassed, but I picked the cross up and examined it with a look of amazement and confusion on my face. 'It can't be, but it is' I stuttered, 'where did you find it'.

Sue then told me that she and Skinny had been going to a busy nightclub called The Rendezvous in Harehills. Walking down the slope she saw something shiny on the floor. She bent down and picked up Terry's cross. It was a great mystery how it had got there, but a miracle that Sue had found it.

Sue was a hard working lady and not one to sit around, So despite her grief and mental anguish, it was not long before she found work. She got a part time job in a cafe on Street Lane in Moortown, Leeds.

One afternoon, they were about to close up for the day, when an old lady came to the door. Without a second thought, Sue let her in and made her a drink and a sandwich.

To Sue's astonishment, the lady said 'I have been sent here from Pontefract' (which is quite a distance away). 'Your name is Sue isn't it'. 'Yes' Sue replied. She carried on to say ' your daughter Terry is stood beside you' then describing her perfectly continued to tell her that she mustn't worry about Terry she was fine where she is but that Terry was worried about her Mum's health. She told Sue to look after herself, and that she was anaemic.

Sue had never met the lady before but thanked her greatly for coming all that way and for the message she had given her.

The conclusions of this story are that if you loose something special there may be a reason. And more importantly that our loved ones are still very much alive and think of us and care about us and sometimes even manage an appearance, or a message.

Nettles one of my favourite herbs

I am still a very passionate advocate of Herbal Medicine and often turn to my favourite herbal 'Bartrams Encyclopaedia of Herbal Medicine', to look for something to help a friend or colleague with their medical condition. Since finding that I was borderline diabetic and for High blood pressure I have treated myself with odourless Garlic capsules and Nettle tea every morning. There has been some improvement and I feel generally healthier. The marvellous thing about herbs is that they very often treat more than one condition and generally have few or no side effects, in fact they have side benefits! I am not advocating avoiding the doctor's surgery, it is always safest to get a professional diagnosis of your condition. Herbs however are a good preventive, supportive and safe medicine. Here are details of conditions and uses of Nettles:

Nettles are high in vitamins including Vitamin C. Serotonin, Histamine, and minerals including iron calcium and Silica.

Actions include Blood tonic, hypoglycaemic, antiseptic, expectorant, vasodilator, circulatory stimulant, re-mineraliser, ant rheumatic, elimination of uric acid, anti-haemorrhagic, mild diuretic also helps increase or reduce flow of breast milk making its own adjustment.

Uses to help with : Iron deficient anaemia, gout, first stage of fevers, Malaria, festering sores, stimulates kidney, de-toxifies blood, uraemia in kidney disease, chronic skin disease, Diabetes, first degree burns and high blood sugar in diabetes. It has the power to eliminate urates and expel gravel, to allay itching of Hodgkin's disease (frequent drinks of nettle tea) Lobster and shell fish allergy, strawberry allergy, and falling hair (tea used as a rinse)

Make a tea with 1oz of herb to a pint of boiling water, infuse for 15mins and drink three times a day.

They can also be bought as capsules or tincture. The boiled leaves can be eaten like spinach.

This is just one example of the many herbs available that have multiple uses.

For difficult cases consult a medical herbalist, or if you are taking other medication check with your doctor that it is safe to use with them.

An important thing to remember is that herbs are generally slow acting and it may take three months or so to see lasting results, so don't give up too soon.

True Colours

Whilst I was living at Harehills, there was a terrible humanitarian crisis in Bangladesh. Great floods had swamped the land and the suffering that had followed was heart-rending.

A friend of mine was collecting items for an auction to raise money for the relief effort. So, joining in I asked a few of my friends if they had anything that they could spare for the auction.

The answers that received told me a lot about them.

The first friend, although she did not have much, showed willing, and collected some things from around her house.

The second, though she had quite a lot of nice possessions said she had nothing to spare.

The third friend, Rose gave me an answer that warmed my heart and showed me what a lovely person she really was.

'June' she said ' This is not my home where I am living, and these are not my things. But if I could I would go there now, because those little babies and children need love as well as everything else'. She spoke with such sincerity and compassion, Rose showed me her true colours and I have always regarded her in high esteem since that day.

Rose was and still is very deep. She once told me that she had miscarried a little baby boy, and one day wrote the most beautiful poem on the attic wall in my house (there was all-sorts of poetry and philosophy written on there) The poem was the story of when she lost her little boy and he took her through the gates of Heaven, but she had to come back. Unfortunately, I have long since moved and Rose can no longer remember all the words, but the memory of it remains.

The consequence of this story is that it is possible to enter Heaven and come back! This is also echoed in Dad's story.

Dad

I have not yet mentioned my Dad in this book. It was not really until I was in my forties that I really appreciated how lucky I was to have a Dad like mine.

He was a very quiet man, my Dad, and quite serious. He did have a sense of humour though, and would laugh raucously at Frankie Howard, Carry on films and the likes, much to my Mums annoyance (mum was a bit more straight laced when it came to vulgar comedy!).

He was a fireman for most of his working life and saw a lot of tragedy.

Dad loved his music, gardening and riding his bike for miles. He was never one to talk about religion much at all. His idea of being close to God was in the garden looking at the flowers or admiring the beautiful scenery of the Yorkshire Dales whilst out on his bike.

It was for this reason it made this story stand out, as it was rare to hear Dad talk about such things.

One of his colleagues in the fire service had been ill for a long time and had slipped into a coma. For three days, his wife sat at his bedside. When he came round and asked for a cup of tea. His wife made him a drink and he said ' I've been to the other side and it was beautiful' He named the six men that he wanted to bear his coffin, one of whom was my Dad. He then slipped peacefully away.

It was not many years after him telling me this story that my Dad himself passed away.

He was only 68 years old, and this particular day he had cycled a long way. He was only five minutes away from home when he suffered a massive heart attack on his bike and died. It was a real shock for us all as he had never been diagnosed with any heart problems.

One of the things that I regret is that no one asked the lovely smart firemen at the funeral to bear his coffin. I am sure Dad is in a beautiful garden now.

The I ching and a Magical Journey

It was whilst I was living at Vicars Terrace that I began to use the I Ching.
A friend of mine had taught me how to use this ancient oracle as a means of divination.
It is a very mysterious book and not easy to use or interpret. The I Ching professes to contain all possibilities and can also be read as a source of wise philosophy. The I Ching was written by the good King Wen in ancient China. Apparently at the time he had been imprisoned by a tyrant. in the 2nd century BC. There are many versions, but I preferred to use the old classic which is a direct translation of the original. I found that it reveals hidden truths and brings understanding and clarity in difficult situations. The reading would often reveal much more than I asked, like a wise all-knowing great spirit watching over me.
My great adventure started when I went to the Glastonbury festival in its early days in 1985.
I had very little money, not even enough to buy my ticket in! and no means of getting there. But I was determined to go. I had lent out my last bit of savings but had been let down. So, respectfully asking the Great Spirit, I concentrated and asked the question 'what would be the outcome if I go to Glastonbury'. Dropping three coins on to the floor six times, I drew a

hexagram. I cannot remember the whole of the text but it was to the effect that I was going with good intentions and that there would be great good fortune!

Leaving the two youngest boys in the care of their Dad and a friend, I set off hitchhiking to Glastonbury from Leeds with young David (aged 7).

I couldn't carry a tent so I asked some neighbours opposite that were going to the festival, if they would transport one down for me and put a notice up on the board when they got there. (these were the days before we all had mobile phones!).

Knowing I had little money, I set off with my favourite herbal, a poetry book and my I Ching with the intentions of bartering for food.

A herbal remedy, poetry recitation or an I Ching reading was what I had to barter with! This would get me through until I could draw a small allowance the following Monday. These were real hippy days!

We were lucky with the lifts and arrived at the site about six hours later. Now we had arrived, but had no money for tickets.

I had planned to collect my tent and camp outside. Heading towards the festival site, I thought I recognised one of the staff at the gate taking tickets as an old friend. I ran towards him and flung my arms around him. Oops! It wasn't my old friend at all, much to his amusement.

I explained about the tent. He gave a quick look around to see that no one was watching and said 'go on in, it doesn't matter about the ticket, just go in'. What a nice young man and a stroke of good luck, or destiny!

There was a sea of people and no sign of a notice board or our tent. So helped by some nice people, we made one out of three thin logs and a thick clear plastic sheet. It was a sort of see though tee pee. We were also fortunate with the weather that year and it was glorious sunshine.

We camped next to a lovely couple with a baby. The lady made little moccasins out of leather and the young Dad had a foot operated jigsaw with which he made things. They were nice people and shared some food with us.

After exploring the site, we snuggled up in our sleeping bags in our makeshift tent and went to sleep.

The next morning, we awoke to another lovely sunny day. It was a beautiful summers day.

I went in search of breakfast for David and me, offering my wares in return. The people on the stalls were lovely and just gave us both a lovely bowl of muesli with fresh fruit.

There were lots of things for kids to do, playgrounds, face painting, music making, and storytelling. The atmosphere was brilliant.

Sometime later that day we met a group of people practising and teaching Raj Yoga, which is a form of meditation. The I Ching had instructed me to look out for a group of people on the hill that were isolated from the rest. They were all very friendly and we spent most of the rest of the festival in their company.

There was one very peculiar incident during this time. We were sat in a tent chatting and somehow the subject had changed to astrology. Someone was talking about Sufism, which is the more mystical side of Islam. In Sufism, they said, there were thirteen sign in the Zodiac, the thirteenth sign being the Arachnid or spider which ran from 26th May to the 10th June. People born under this sign were supposed to encompass all the signs of the zodiac and were supposed to weave people together.

One by one we revealed that we were born the 5th, 6th, 7th and 8th of June. I have no idea what the odds of that happening are! Meanwhile, David was sat in the corner of the tent sketching and had drawn a picture of a woman and turned it into a spider.

As the festival was drawing to an end, Martin who was also interested in the meditation and whom we had made friends with, invited us to go to London. So we joined him and went to see my sister Hazel who lived in Wimbledon.

My sister was surprised to see us and made us very welcome. We accompanied Martin to a Raj Yoga meeting in London not far from where my sister lived.

Everyone was dressed in white, and a lady called Dadi Janki (who is now 100 years old and still teaching) spoke a guided meditation. It was so peaceful; the room was filled with love.

Martin invited us to go back to Glastonbury with him to camp. I loved the place so much but was worried about my other children back in Leeds. I asked the 'Great spirit' through the I Ching. It said not to worry, that everything would be fine.

So off we went back to Glastonbury.

We arrived back and found a camp site in a farmer's field right under the famous Glastonbury Tor. For those not familiar, the Tor is an ancient landmark and is steeped in legends. From the top you can see for at least 20 miles in all directions. It is a famous place of pilgrimage for many, including saints.

The following morning our new friend Martin, David and myself walked into the centre of Glastonbury. There was a meditation session being held above an old library. There we met Michael George. He was to conduct the meditation lesson. He seemed very pleasant and modest, and was softly spoken and easy to approach.

There were twenty or so people in the room. David sat quietly with his sketch pad and pencils.

Michael talked us through a meditation practice (which is done with eyes open), whilst gentle relaxing music played in the background. Again it was very tranquil and I saw light which seemed not to be of this world.

After the talk, we went downstairs and into a very old cobbled courtyard where there was an open air cafe. As David and I sat with a drink and a snack we were joined by a lady. She had long blond wavy hair and I would say she was in her thirties.

The lady was talking to David when all of a sudden he said out of the blue 'I know where the sword is. It's buried under a little tree in the shade of a big tree'.

As you may know, the legend of King Arthur's sword, Excalibur is centred around Glastonbury.

In itself what David had said meant very little, except that I had not told him about that legend. But to my surprise the lady replied, 'I know where that place is, I had a dream about it when I first moved to Glastonbury'.

At that point a tall dark bearded gentleman came over, who was obviously acquainted with the lady. This seemed to disturb the conversation, but before the lady left she gave David a silver propelling pencil with an Amethyst encased in the end of the shaft.

To this day I still wonder if we could go back and find the lady and Excalibur. Indeed, it would be miraculous. I wonder what power the sword contains, and what would happen if it were found.

We returned to the camp on the hillside and started chatting. I said to David 'You know when we were in that room, I saw a lot of beautiful light, did you see anything'. 'Oh yes' David replied in a very matter of fact manner, 'I was walking on water'. My jaw nearly dropped to the ground. I was speechless.

The following day was to be just as mysterious. We met up with Michael George in Glastonbury. He was very modest and seemed very ordinary, until you asked him questions!

It seems he had practiced Raj Yoga meditation for many years, rising early every morning to meditate and adhering to a strict diet.

In short he had decided to dedicate his life to the practice and teaching of Raj Yoga. In fact he is still teaching and writing books now, some thirty years later.

One thing that he told me truly astonished me. He said that he could draw himself out of his body through here, pointing at the place that we call the third eye (this place is regarded by Raj Yoga as the seat of the soul). He said he could then travel anywhere in the universe at the speed of thought. This claim was not made boastfully. Though it may seem beyond belief, it is supported by the writings of other Yogi's and Michael seemed completely genuine.

That day we decided to climb the Tor and set off up the steep hillside, Michael, Martin, David, myself and another young man who's name I can't remember, who was also learning about meditation.

We climbed the Tor, but the weather had changed since we set off. It was now quite blustery. We wondered around at the top for a few minutes taking in the scenery and then made our way back down.

When we got back to the tent I cast an I Ching reading.

Again my jaw dropped in amazement as I read 'They went up the mountain, they came down the mountain, they could have illuminated the four corners of the universe'.

I took this to mean that if we had all meditated at the top of the Tor, it would have had an extremely magical effect. It is a place where many ley lines converge, and where many saints have trod. Some believe that the veil between Heaven and Earth is thinner in such places. Who knows what could have happened?

The opportunity had passed for us, but come on you Yogi's, if you are reading this book, go ahead and do it! I am sure it is still possible.

That was the last of my experiences in Glastonbury, but not the last of Raj Yoga.

Martin had to leave and took me and David a good distance towards home. I returned glowing. I had never felt as healthy in all my life.

The consequence of this story are very far reaching. That Excalibur is real and still could be found. That children like David may be more sensitive to meditation and mystical experiences. Also that through meditation we could light up the world! and that through strict practice of Raj Yoga you can train yourself to travel out of your body to anywhere in the universe at the speed of thought. Quite a claim, but how many of us have the discipline and will to do it? Also, that there are some very magical places on the Earth. Another place that has the same feel is the Holy Island, Lindisfarne.

Legends Of glastonbury

Joseph of Arimathea (who purchased the cave for Christ's burial) was believed to have travelled to England with the Holy Grail, the cup of Christ from the last supper. The legend is that it is buried somewhere in Glastonbury and that only the truly righteous would ever find it.

Legend is that he stuck his staff into the ground and as he slept it sprouted and was known for many years as the Christ thorn. It was only replaced recently when the original tree died in a drought.

The other great legend is of course that Excalibur the magical sword of the great King Arthur is to be found there.

There is much to support this legend as the grave of King Arthur was indeed discovered by monks at Glastonbury Abbey in 1190ad.

Glastonbury is believed to be the site of the first Christian church, made of 'wattle and daub' in the grounds of the present Glastonbury Abbey. The Tor itself was apparently once paved, and is the centre of many legends.

June's 'Tribe'

Left to right: David, Rosie, June, Brendan, Sam & Michael.

David & Michael

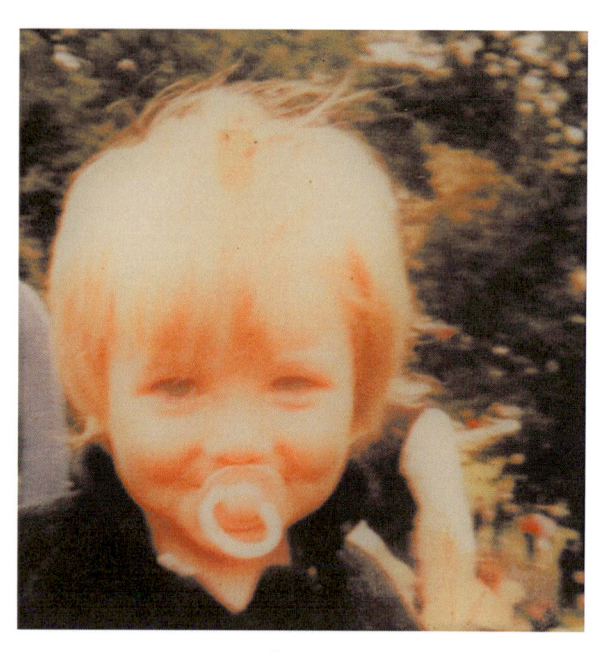

Sam

Brendan & Rose

Twins Gillian & Marian

Michael Brendan David & Sam

An Unexpected Healing

Back in Leeds, life went on. It was a busy house with many visitors.

This particular day something quite extraordinary happened.

In one of the attic rooms we had a sitting room. One sunny afternoon we had a few friends around. I can't remember if it was a special occasion, but there were about 8 or so visitors.

We were all sat chatting and the kids were playing. Suddenly David came to me in obvious pain holding his back. He had been clowning around doing tipple overs and had really hurt himself.

Everybody was still talking. I got quite upset, Seeing David was in agony and shouted 'be quiet everyone David has hurt his back'.

Amongst the friends and visitors that day was a young man called Paul, who lived in the next street. Paul was perhaps in his late twenties, quite attractive and softly spoken (he incidentally claimed to be the first ever black male stripper!).

Paul came over and picked David up in his arms, reassuring him that he would be alright.

He carried David to a mattress on the floor and laid him down. The room was silent. Paul knelt over David and moved his hands in a pattern above him but not touching. David fell to sleep, waking about 5 minutes later he was absolutely fine.

The conclusion of this story is that the most unexpected people may have divine gifts, we should never 'judge a book by its cover'.

The Healer

Is anybody happier because you passed this way?
Does anybody remember that you spoke to them today?
Can you say tonight in parting with a day that's slipping fast
That you helped a single brother in the many that you passed?
Is a single heart rejoicing over what you said or did?
Does a man who's hopes were fading now with courage look ahead?
As you close your eyes in slumber, do you think that God will say,
You have earned one more tomorrow by the work you did today.

This poem reminds me so much of Mum and her lovely ways. Always thoughtful and compassionate. Her days were full of good deeds and kind words.

Little Claire

I made many friends and met many interesting characters in Chapeltown, it was a real melting pot of different cultures and people.

I became friends with a lady called Margret, who was from the same housing co-operative as me. Margret was a single Mum of three, and the youngest was called Claire. Claire was a really bonny little girl; she had pale brown skin, lovely blue eyes and a mop of ginger curly hair. Claire had downs syndrome and unfortunately also suffered from a lot of chest infections.

Sadly, at the age of three Claire got pneumonia and the hospital could not save her despite their best attempts. Little Claire passed away. I tried to comfort Margaret the best I could as did many of her other friends and relatives.

When I went to visit Margaret a few weeks later, she told me that she regularly saw Claire playing around the house with some other spirit children. How lovely.

Eventually some months later Margaret had been thinking about moving home. She really wanted to move but she was so worried that she would not see Claire any more. I reassured her that Claire was with her not with the house.

Eventually Margaret did move house, and when I bumped into her one day on the bus to town she said that she still saw Claire and her little playmates at their new home.

Magical Brahma Kumaris

After yet another disastrous relationship, I moved with the three boys to Hamilton Avenue in Chapeltown. It was there that I got in touch with a lady called Ross who lived some distance away in Village square near Burley.

She was a teacher of Raj Yoga and I decided to take up the course of six lessons that she offered. All lessons were free of charge.

There was only a small group of people at Ross's house for the course (about five or so). The weekly lessons began with a bit of background and philosophy. Their belief is that all religions came at different times to fulfil the needs of that time, like branches of the same tree. We were taught simple open eyed meditation. Concentrating on a simple mandala or pattern, which you try to keep your focus on the centre, and also try to look as though you are seeing from the third eye (seat of the soul).

We learnt a simple verse to say over to yourself (either inwardly or out loud) which helps you to focus your thoughts and empower your soul. I say this verse over to myself whilst concentrating on a mandala.

I am a peaceful soul
I am situated just above and behind the centre of the eyes
My original qualities are peace, power, love and light.

You can try this for yourself using the mandala printed in the book.

The mind is very restless and wanders off all the time. Just be patient with yourself and keep going back to the centre and the verse. I have used this meditation many times since and have seen the room glow with light.

Magical things seemed to happen around these lessons. One day I had been to a lesson when I found that the weather had changed. When I came out of Ross's house and made my way to the bus stop it became cold and windy.

'Brrr' I said to myself 'God why have you left me so cold'.

I turned my head and to my astonishment, across the back of a bench there was a cream woollen jumper with its arms outstretched! I looked around and there was no one in sight. I put the jumper on and proceeded on my journey as warm as toast!

On another occasion, I set off for a lesson and had no bus fare home. Ross said she could not lend me the money for my fare. She was so sorry but it was their policy. So accepting this, I set off to walk home. After walking a couple of miles, I arrived at the ridge of Meanwood Valley. It was a lovely warm sunny day and as I sat down to have a rest, I drifted off to sleep.

I had a strange dream in which I was told that I had two things to overcome, laziness and greed.

It was about right! I have definitely conquered the laziness now but still have some way to go with the greed. All these temptations!

On a third occasion I had set off from Chapeltown to Harehills to catch a bus that would take me all the way through town to Burley and would get me to Ross's house on time.

I had decided to wear a long white dress with red embroidery around it that my sister had given to me. Time was getting on and as I was hurrying. I could see the bus at the other side of the road pulling away from the bus stop. I was just about to stop and turn back when the bus screeched to a halt and waited. I ran and jumped on the bus. It turned out that my brother (who rarely caught the bus to town) had been on the bus and spotted me running and asked the driver to stop the bus for me.

There is definitely something special about Brahma Kumaris the organisation that teaches Raj Yoga and there were to be many more magical things to come. Even now I can sit in a room and meditate and the whole room lights up.

The Mormons

During the next few years I settled into a steady relationship. At least it was to begin with! I had my fourth boy Brendan Francis whilst I lived in Bramley in Leeds followed a year later by Rose-Marie my first girl. Finally moving back to Seacroft I fell pregnant again.

I hardly dare tell my Mum! It turned out I was having twins. I was lucky with the births and delivered two healthy babies with the assistance of the wonderful doctors and nurses at St James hospital. They were named Gillian Hazel and Marian Dawn. Now there were seven!

June with twins two days old

It was at that house in Seacroft that the missionaries came knocking at our door. They were really nice people, very genuine and my friend Lesley and I joined the church and were members for quite a few years. We even got baptised by full immersion.

Unfortunately, my relationship with my partner went badly. During the years we were together the father of the youngest four (who was a clever and a talented artist) was in and out of addiction problems, and despite my attempts to get him sorted out I ultimately failed. We parted after a very unpleasant incident.

The church was very supportive and helpful (as was my friend Lesley). But as I got deeper into the philosophy I found it confusing and really not for me. Even so, I still have the greatest respect for the Mormon Church whose real title is The Church of Jesus Christ of Latter Day Saints. I was impressed how the leaders were not paid and how they gave a lot to charity without boasting about it (they are the world's biggest contributors to the Red Cross). They also taught the Word of Wisdom, which was a guide given by their prophet that made a lot of sense.

Extract from the word of wisdom,

5 That inasmuch as any man drinketh wine or strong drink among you, behold it is not good, neither meet in the sight of your Father, only in assembling yourselves together to offer up your sacraments before him.

6 And, behold, this should be wine, yea, pure wine of the grape of the vine, of your own make.

7 And, again, strong drinks are not for the belly, but for the washing of your bodies.

8 And again, tobacco is not for the body, neither for the belly, and is not good for man, but is an herb for bruises and all sick cattle, to be used with judgment and skill.

9 And again, hot drinks are not for the body or belly.

10 And again, verily I say unto you, all wholesome herbs God hath ordained for the constitution, nature, and use of man—

11 Every herb in the season thereof, and every fruit in the season thereof; all these to be used with prudence and thanksgiving.

12 Yea, flesh also of beasts and of the fowls of the air, I, the Lord, have ordained for the use of man with thanksgiving; nevertheless, they are to be used sparingly;

13 And it is pleasing unto me that they should not be used, only in times of winter, or of cold, or famine.

14 All grain is ordained for the use of man and of beasts, to be the staff of life, not only for man but for the beasts of the field, and the fowls of heaven, and all wild animals that run or creep on the earth;

15 And these hath God made for the use of man only in times of famine and excess of hunger.

16 All grain is good for the food of man; as also the fruit of the vine; that which yieldeth fruit, whether in the ground or above the ground—

This may well have been inspired. The word of Wisdom was written in the eighteen hundreds when little was known about the dangers of drink and tobacco. Many people don't like the restrictive nature of religious teachings but if you look at them as trying to guide and protect us rather than to punish and deny us pleasure they often make sense.

Mums True Love

Throughout this period, Mum was very much a Spiritualist. She had a few interesting encounters with spirit. This is one that she told me about.

When Mum was a young 18-year-old country girl, she was very much in love and engaged to be married to a young man called Ian. Ian road a motorbike, and tragically he was killed in a crash.

My Mum's heart was broken. I don't think she was ever able to love anyone as deeply as she loved him.

Many years later, when we were all grown up, she had gone to stay with a friend, an old lady called Mrs Hill who lived a few streets away in Whinmoor, Leeds. As they lay in twin beds, Mum and Mrs hill both saw Ian walk down between them. A few days later they both saw Ian sat in an armchair. Mum said that he did not look like a ghost at all, but that he appeared to be just real as you and me! Mrs Hill could also see him very clearly and described his clothing and appearance to my Mum.

During the same period that Mum lived in Whinmoor, she set up a Healing Centre at Seacroft library in Leeds. There were usually two or three healers working, and the doors were open for anyone to come in and be given healing for free.

Many people came. Some were healed, or experienced great improvement, and many were comforted and felt great peace. It was called The Haven of Light. There was always a lovely friendly welcoming atmosphere, and the people were very down to earth. Mum kept the healing centre going for a number of years until circumstances changed and she could no longer manage it. Mum still occasionally gave healing at 85 years old!, often while she was working in our charity shop if it was quiet and someone is in pain. She was a real character and an inspiration much loved in our community. We really miss her.

My friends Jo and Zacka/Krishna

One day I had a call from my friend Jo More, who is a Homeopath. Her relationship had come to an end and she needed a hand moving. So I went to meet her with a friend Mo, to give her a helping hand. As we approached the house she was moving to, there was a chap with his back turned to us and one trouser leg rolled up, tinkering with an old VW camper van. He introduced himself as Zacka and said he was a friend of Jo's.

We all went inside and chatted, it was decided I would go with Zacka for some company in his VW to pick some furniture up.

'Your friend has an interesting aura' he said 'she has put up a brick wall'. Poor Mo was a bit of an emotional wreck at the time so I'm sure that this was right. We chatted away and somehow I started telling him all my recent problems. 'What do you do for a living' I said. He reached over into the glove compartment and handed me a leaflet.

I was well impressed! He did counselling, massage and healing. 'You must be a good counsellor; "I've just told you all my problems" I said. He had a lovely smile and as my daughters would say, he was 'well fit'! As we got out of the van and along the path he did a backwards somersault in the air, impressive I thought, I struggled to do a forward roll at school!

We helped a tearful Jo pack and returned to her new gaff. When we arrived at Jo's we unpacked and had a cuppa.

As we left Zacka gave me a kiss on the cheek. 'You jammy bitch' Mo said outside. I thought nothing of the kiss, as, I thought he was way out of my league.

I decided to have some counselling sessions with Zacka as I had been through some very difficult stuff. Even though I thought he was gorgeous it was still a very difficult thing. On the last visit I had a massage, the best I've ever had. I was so relaxed I felt like I was floating weightless on a cloud.

Zacka never spoke much about his beliefs, but Zacka was a given name, and he was then given the name Krishna, presumably by the religious order that he belonged to.

One day Krishna gave me a lift home, he was selling up and going away for a while and I had bought a few things from him.

On the way he invited me to go to the Glastonbury festival with him. My favourite place, I would have loved to go, but at the time I was still getting visits from the social welfare because of trouble with my previous partner so I was afraid to leave the kids in the care of my friend, and had to say no.

We stood in front of my house to say our goodbyes. 'I hope you find someone nice or nobody at all' I said 'I was just about to say the same thing to you' I replied. We had a big hug and a kiss and as I turned to go in Krishna said 'Wow I don't know what you are doing but it must be right, very, very right, the whole street has lit up'.

In conclusion, we all have an Aura which shows our souls energy, and that Love can light up the world.

'Freedom and love go together. Love is not a reaction. If I love you because you love me, that is a mere trade, a thing to be bought in the market: it is not love. To love is not to ask anything in return, not even to feel that you are giving something, and it is only such love that can know freedom' - Jiddu Krishnamurti

'Our freedom lies in remaining open continuously, not only to life's changes but to the divine light within us and others' - Peter Santos

My Healing Experiences

Shortly after the last episode, whilst living in Seacroft I met Leon. He came to our house to repair the kid's PlayStation after contacting him through a newspaper advertisement.

I talked to him in the same friendly manner as I would any visitor and made him a cuppa and chatted whilst he mended the machine. I noticed he had bad psoriasis on his elbows and I offered to try and find a remedy to help with it. He left with a smile and I thought nothing more of it.

A week or so after his first visit I called him to order some games. Much to my surprise, on his return he burst into the house full of joy and announced that he had fallen in love with me the first time we met!

This was most unexpected. I decided, well this is different, maybe he will be ok, so we became friends. He would use any excuse or opportunity to come and see me. Leon was in an unhappy marriage and after much wooing on his part, our friendship turned to romance.

Relationships of this kind were strictly forbidden in the Mormon Church, so on the advice of the bishop (who was a lovely man) I left rather than be excommunicated!

Even now I can see the sense in this. People got hurt. There is still a part in my conscience that says I should have encouraged him to go back to his wife and children and make a go of it. However, the romance turned into a relationship and Leon eventually moved in with our family.

A couple of months down the line I saw a weekend course in Reiki healing advertised and decided to go along.

I had practiced some healing at the centre with my Mum but was curious to know more.

There were only three of us on the course and two teachers. We were taught the background, theories and symbols of Reiki. We also had our chakra's (centres of energy within the body) opened.

We practised healing on each other and on the teachers, passing our hands over the body of the patient, but not touching. I noticed there was a strange tingling sensation in my hands in some places which invariably turned out to be a site of pain or where there was an old injury. We were taught to channel healing energy through our hands and to remove negative energy. It was fascinating. We were presented with certificates though I felt that we weren't properly qualified.

I went home. The first opportunity to practice was on Leon's head. He said that it felt strange, like his brain had been de-fragmented (like when a computer sorts all its files out and puts them in order). The next day I also put my hands on the soles of his feet, he said he could feel the healing energy filling up his body.

In the next few weeks there was to be another miracle of healing.

Seacroft was a bit of a rough area, and whilst there were some great characters, there were some on the scary side.

There was an incident one day when a rough looking young man came to the door asking for one of my lads friends. Leon seemed to think he wanted to cause trouble. He shouted at him and got his multi tool out of his back pocket. This was a bad move. The lad scarpered shouting that he would be back with his brothers. When my boys found out they said 'You must be crazy Leon, that family have got shooters'.

We concluded that if they returned, Leon would have to take a beating, or it might escalate into something much worse.

Two big lads returned shouting that Leon had threatened their brother with a knife. They dragged Leon into the garden and punched and kicked him.

I was yelling at them to stop and they did eventually.

Leon was in pain, his front tooth was loose and bleeding and he was clutching his ribs.

A few days later his tooth had settled down and healed but he was still in a lot of pain with his ribs. I felt really sorry for him and put my hands gently on his ribs and silently prayed for him to be healed (I remember I also promised God that I would stop smoking if he healed him! a promise that I later broke).

As I came to the end of my prayer, I closed with ' I ask this in the name of Jesus Christ, amen'. As I said this, in fact at the precise moment I said Jesus Christ, I felt a strange sensation where my fingers were, like bones moving. Leon's eyes opened wide and he sat bolt upright and stared at me. 'It's gone' he exclaimed 'the pains gone'. He was amazed, I was pretty amazed myself.

The following day Leon was still feeling some pain in the same area. He said nothing to me about it, but had thought to himself 'I bet she can't heal that last bit of pain'. Well higher forces must definitely have been at work. Without saying a word, I put my hand in the same place and prayed. The pain completely disappeared. Leon was again amazed and told me what he had been thinking.

Over the years I had a few more experiences of healing but I don't think any were quite as profound as this. It honestly seemed as though his bones had knitted back together with the power of healing.

The Bible on healing

Healing used to be very much a part of the Christian church service, I don't know why it is not practised so much now in churches, but it was very much part of Christ's will that his disciples should heal the sick.

Mathew10;v1- 'And he called unto him his twelve disciples, he gave them power against unclean spirits, to cast them out, and to heal all manner of sickness, and all manner of disease'.

Mathew 10; v8-'Heal the sick, cleanse the lepers, raise the dead, cast out devils, freely you have received, freely give'.

James 5: v14-'Is there any sick amongst you? Let him call for the elders of the church: and let them pray over him, anointing him with oil in the name of the Lord' (this is also still practiced in the Mormon church)

My friend Jenny

It was while I was living in Seacroft that I met up with Jenny, a Zambian lady who was to become a big part of my life. I met Jenny though her brother Vincent who was a close friend from the Mormon church. Vincent had become extremely ill, and being a widow with three girls to support, the church asked his sister to come all the way from Zambia to care for him and the children. There was a very real fear that Vincent might pass away and the children would be left orphaned.

Jenny did a splendid job, and after many months of care and nursing Vincent regained his health.

By this time Jenny and I had become great friends. We shared our joys and our sorrows (and still do!).

I would like to share this story she told me, which I found really amusing.

Uncle's Ghost- (not really!)

When Jenny was very young, one of her uncle's from a distant village passed away.

In the tradition of Zambia, all the children of the family would go to stay with the remaining relative so that they were not lonely. So Jenny was taken to her Aunt's house. The people in the Zambian villages are very poor, and Jenny had to sleep on a rush mat on the floor with her cousin.

They only had one blanket between them and it was pretty cool in the evening. As the lay on the floor dozing, Jenny's cousin kept pulling the blanket off her and Jenny kept pulling it back. Jenny was getting more and more tired and cross and eventually she snapped. Turning to her cousin who was wrapped in the blanket sleeping, Jenny slapped her hard on the face, and laid back down quickly, wrapping the blanket her. She laid there motionless.

Her cousin woke up startled and started screaming, believing that the ghost of her uncle had returned and slapped her!

Such a commotion ensued, before long the whole household was awake and scared.

Jenny stayed quiet, she knew that she would be in terrible trouble if she admitted what she had done.

The longer it went on, the harder it became to tell the truth.

Even to the day she told me the story, she had not owned up to her aunt. Naughty Jenny!

A Priceless Gift

Friendship is a priceless gift
That can't be bought or sold,
But its value is far greater
Than a mountain made of gold.

So when you ask God for a gift,
Be thankful that he sends,
Not diamonds, pearls, or riches,
But the love of a real, true friend.

From a poem by Helen Steiner Rice

My Dear Friend Lesley

I had some good friends and neighbours in Seacroft, in particular Lesley Stone who was a great friend and regular visitor. We looked after each other quite a lot, especially through the time when I was a single mum. I would frequently cook her tea and she would look after the kids when I needed. Lesley was good company. Having a good babysitter also meant that I could go to college part time on an evening, which I really enjoyed.

All was well, and it was a really happy household on the whole until one day, out of the blue, my x partner and father of the four youngest kids, showed up at the house, drunk, and mentally very unstable.

We had parted in very unpleasant circumstances.

The neighbours helped to see him off and I called the police.

I felt very vulnerable afterwards. I was afraid that he might come back and try to abduct one of the children. The incident upset me so much that I decided that the only way we would be safe was to leave the area completely and move to somewhere That my 'x' was unlikely to find us.

I promised the kids we would find somewhere nice, but it wasn't going to be easy with such a big family.

I went to the local council, but the stock of large council houses was very limited.

After some weeks of looking they offered us a house in Fagley, Bradford, but when we went to view it, it was a great disappointment. It was a worse estate than Seacroft. The house at either side was boarded up and a horse was tethered in the back garden. Some loudmouth shouted from the top of the street 'you'll be all right ere love, there's no Paki's round ere'.

This was not what I wanted, as we came away I fought back the tears. I had promised the kids we would move somewhere nice, and this very definitely wasn't it.

I returned home, wondering what on earth to do. I felt unsafe where we were but we didn't have much money behind us and our options were limited. That evening I read my stars in the Evening Post. I don't usually take much heed to them, but on this occasion the advice stuck in my head. 'Do not be railroaded in to taking something you do not want' my stars said. This influenced me to decide to keep looking.

During the next week or so I somehow came across a leaflet from the Key House Project in Keighley. It had houses to rent from landlords who were willing accept DHSS clients. There was a four bedroomed house advertised in a place called Denholme which I had never heard of. Leon took me to view it.

When we arrived at the village, we were met by a lovely friendly landlady. The house we had come to view was a big old stone built terrace house with a roaring coal fire. It was the answer to my prayers.

We signed up for the house and moved in, in December 1999, just before Christmas and the Millennium celebrations. The two oldest boys, now young men decided to stay in Seacroft, but eventually moved To Denholme.

The kids settled in Schools and we were even lucky enough to rent a smallholding with two cats, ducks, hens and a couple of sheep.

We had not been in Denholme for many months when we got some very sad news. My dear friend Lesley had died suddenly and had been found by her only son John. We were all really sad. Lesley was only in her forties.

John her son was only 18, so myself and a few other friends rallied round and helped John to organise the funeral. All along I felt really guilty that I hadn't been to see her since I moved. I felt that I had let her down.

One day Lesley was very much on my mind. I went upstairs to have a shower, but overcome with emotion, I started weeping and quietly saying my sorrys to her.

I heard her voice, her lovely soft Lancashire accent 'Don't be so daft' she said 'I'm fine, I am happy where I am'.

I still missed Lesley for a long time, but felt much better knowing she was happy. We planted a yellow rose bush in her memory.

The consequence of this story is that loved ones that have passed know when you are thinking about them, and they draw near to you.

Quick trip to Heaven!

I continued with evening classes at college in Keighley doing an RSA in counselling and another course in Aromatherapy massage. I really enjoyed college and met some nice and interesting friends during this time.

During this period, when talking about meditation to my friend Heather. One day, we decided to go to a talk and meditation session in Leeds which was being held by Brahma Kumaris.

We went along to a busy community Hall in Leeds, where we were all welcomed and given a little slip of paper with a spiritual message on.

The talk and meditation practice went on, this time to quite a large audience of around 50 people from all backgrounds. Again I felt peaceful and saw beautiful light.

The surprise came when I asked my friend what she had experienced. In a very 'matter of fact' manner she said 'Well I went through these three circles of Light and then I was in this beautiful garden'.

I was amazed.

In conclusion, some people are much more open to spiritual experiences. I am sure on this occasion my friend was transported straight to Heaven.

On Death

You would know the secret of death.
But how shall you find it unless you seek it in the heart of life?
The owl whose night-bound eyes are blind unto the day cannot unveil the mystery of light.
If you would indeed behold the spirit of death, open your heart wide unto the body of life.
For life and death are one, even as the river and the sea are one.

In the depth of your hopes and desires lies your silent knowledge of the beyond;
And like seeds dreaming beneath the snow your heart dreams of spring.
Trust the dreams, for in them is hidden the gate to eternity.

Extract from Kahlil Gibran 'On Death'

Spurred Into Action

In 2002 whilst living in George Street, I regularly rang my Zambian friend Jenny in Leeds. Sometimes we would make a Sunday dinner and take it over to her, which she really appreciated.

One particular day I could hear a great sadness in her voice. 'What's wrong Jenny, you sound really down' I enquired.

'It's my Mum and Dad' she replied 'They have no food; I am afraid that they might die of starvation'. 'There is a drought in Zambia, the animals are dying the crops have failed, there is starvation, there have been no proper rains in two years'

I was stunned. I had heard of many disasters over the years, but none had hit me quite like this one, this was very personal My friend's parents could starve to death.

We had to do something.

We were not well off ourselves but we gathered what little money we could spare and sent it by Western Union to Jenny's parents so that they could travel to buy food. Knowing that that would not be anywhere near enough I started thinking of other ways of raising money when I spotted a pile of things being thrown out of a house where there had been a flood.

Plucking up courage I knocked on the door and asked if they would mind if I took them to do a car boot sale for Africa. They said I was welcome, so I took them home.

Designer clothes were washed and ironed, amongst the heap of things there was jewellery and other good items.

I started asking around my friends, family and neighbours. Soon we had enough for a car boot stall.

So it began. We formed a small group and called ourselves Mpika Relief Fund. Mpika being the village in Zambia where Jenny's parents lived.

The money we raised was sent through to the church in Mpika to buy food for the local people.

A year or so passed and things started to improve in Zambia. The rains came and things returned to normal (though the people were still very poor).

I thought it was a shame to leave it at that.

We had a good little group of people helping.

Being the time that the AIDS crisis was in the headlines, my thoughts turned to the orphans. 'Have you ever thought of running an orphanage' I said to Jenny one day. 'It's what I have always dreamt of doing' Jenny replied. 'Right then we will do it' I said naively, thinking it would be easy! Starting with a small room in the village of Denholme we began to set up our premises. Friends and neighbours helped us to get the room into a fit state to use as a shop and charitable status came through on November 4th 2002, the day we were due to open. Customers and donated goods started to flow in and out, and soon we had a lovely little community shop which I have really loved running.

Jenny was well qualified for the job of running an orphanage. Back home she had worked as a nurse, midwife, health educator and a hospital administrator. She contacted her family and colleagues back in Mpika and they Began to form a commitee and look for potential sites for the orphanage.

With much hard work and help from some lovely people we now have a beautiful, loving orphanage, a wonderful school and a farm in Mpika. We also help the wider community there.

In Yorkshire we have a fantastic team of people who keep running a shop and a furniture warehouse as well as having child sponsors and events.

I have met some wonderful people whilst doing this work and it has enriched my life greatly. Our project continues to run and is at present still run entirely by volunteers.

You can look us up on line at www.mpika.org.

"The best way to find yourself is to lose yourself in the service of others."

Mahatma Ghandi

Photos of our orphanage and school

Mpika Village of Hope Orphanage

Jenny and baby Connor.

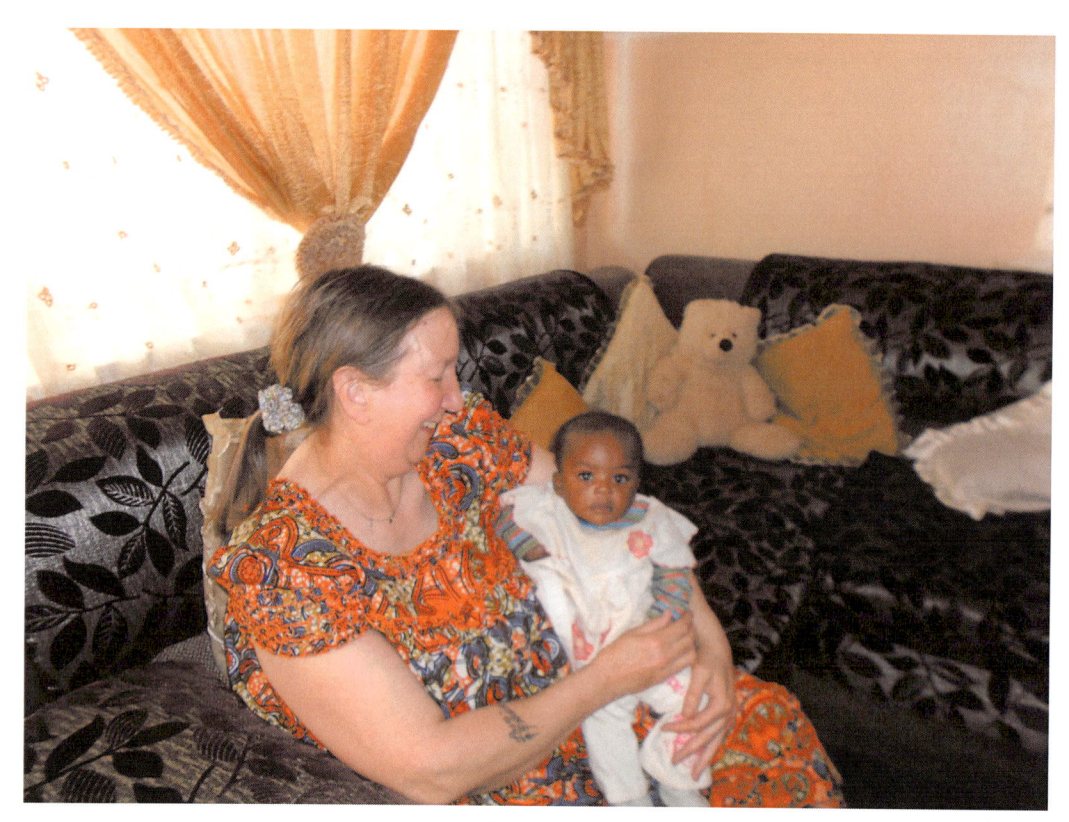

June and baby Dorothy

Children in orphanage lounge

children dancing and singing.

Children at our school

children having lunch

three of our lovely girls

This is a poem I wrote for Jenny, upon hearing of the death of her lovely sister Veronica.

<u>Veronica</u>

Think of me not in pain and sorrow
For my pain has melted like the winter snow when spring has come
And Joy has melted all my sorrow away
Think of me not as the cold corpse now lying in the ground
This is my old body, which now I have left behind like a chrysalis from which a butterfly has emerged, anew and beautiful I have flown away.
Think of me not in the sick bed, for I am no longer there,
I am in the most beautiful garden full of flowers of every colour, and I am smiling.
Think of me not as lost and gone forever, for I am with you when you think of me with love, our hearts are still joined as there is no distance that love cannot travel.
I have made my journey, as you too will one day, and when that day comes I will be waiting to greet you.

June Martin

The Reading at Strawberry Cottage

My friend from college, Lynne, and I were talking one day about mediums and we decided to book a reading.

I had heard of a medium called Shirley Emsley who had a good reputation as being both accurate and genuine so I rang and arranged for her to join us both at Lynne's house, Strawberry Cottage, near Keighley.

We both had an hour reading which was recorded and given to us later on a disc. Shirley read my Tarot cards and gave me lots of information about what I was going to do with my life. She said she could see lots of children and money coming in. She had not been told at the time that I was raising money to build an orphanage in Zambia. She also brought up relationship problems and told me that we would separate but that Leon would be fine.

I swapped places with Lynne. So that she could have some privacy I sat upstairs in one of the bedrooms.

Lynne had a strong spirit presence that came through to her 'He says he's not ginger he's strawberry blond' Shirley said 'This young man ended his life tragically' she went on. 'He says he has a connection with your name that used to be a joke'.

Lynne was astounded. Her old school friend who had been a childhood boyfriend had recently taken his life. His surname was Lynne and they used to joke that if they ever got married she would be Lynne Lynne! He always said he was strawberry blonde not ginger! Shirley went on to give more details of the events around his death, and why he took his life.

Lynne was also told that she would meet someone through work and that they would have a child, which eventually came to pass

We were both very impressed by Shirley, she had given accurate details, not vagaries, things she could not have known.

In conclusion, there are some good and accurate mediums out there who can genuinely communicate between us and souls who have passed away. Unfortunately, not all are genuine so be careful who you consult.

My Other little Boy

Life has a way of giving you surprises, and this was one of my biggest.

Four or more years into my relationship with Leon (I was now 46 and my youngest the twins were twelve) I felt as though I might be pregnant. It seemed unlikely, as years before Leon had 'the snip' when his former wife had trouble in childbirth and had nearly lost her own life.

When we first got together I had said that if I fell pregnant it would be a miracle and would be meant to happen.

The signs got stronger and by now I had missed a period and my breasts were feeling tender. Sure enough when I used the pregnancy testing kit the magic two lines appeared.

Sadly, Leon did not feel the same way and sank into a deep depression, saying he was not well enough and too old to make a good father.

It was a very difficult time for me but nothing anyone would have said would have made me consider having an abortion. I had decided, I would make it through even if it was to be without the father.

One evening however things took a different turn. I ran a bath for Leon's aches and pains and put some essential oils in. I got in the bath too not realising the danger.

That night I started spotting bright red blood. I went to the doctors the next day and they sent me for a scan.

There was no heartbeat. I had miscarried. I later discovered that the Juniper oil that I had put in the bath probably caused the miscarriage, it should never be used during pregnancy.

I was in the very early stages of pregnancy, and with the rest of my family around me, I soon came to terms with what had happened.

I was very sad to have lost the baby, but if I am to be honest I was also a bit relieved as I knew it would have been very hard for me.

A few years later, Mum invited me and a friend Sandra to the oldest Spiritualist Church in England situated in Ebor Street, Keighley.

They were having a special fundraising day.

We each paid a small donation and then picked a name out of a bag.

The name you picked determined the medium that you got to spend 30 or so minutes with in a private reading. I was directed to a smart young man, I can't remember his name now but he was quietly spoken and had a kind face. The first thing he said was 'I've got a little boy here, he must be only about three years old. He's full of emotion'.

'He is coming towards you carrying a candle to light your way, can you accept this'. 'Yes', I said. I knew it was my little boy. The young man also brought through other friends that had passed away, including my friend Cathy from church in Leeds. Cathy was born with Spina bifida and had spent most of her life in a wheelchair. She was tiny, with a big personality and great sense of humour. The young psychic also kept on insisting that there was a black and white dog that kept coming. I kept saying no I didn't have a black and white dog. The dog I had all the waythrough the children's childhood was a black and tan dog called Sunny. The penny finally dropped, the dog was Sam a short haired border collie who had belonged to an old Yorkshireman called Jack who I had cleaned for many years and had become very close to. Jack was like a grandad to me, and I was very upset when he passed away.

When the session was finished I shook the young mans hand and thanked him then went to join my Mum and Sandra.

We left the church and headed for a local pub (not usual for us!). Sandra needed a stiff drink, she was told in the reading that her troubles were far from over, which also sadly proved to be right.

The Story of Jack

Jack was like the Grandad I never had (both my Grandads died before I was born). He lived in a 'granny flat', besides his daughters (our landladies) house.

I would go to do his cleaning once a week. An hour chatting and an hours cleaning was the usual!. He was smashing though and always full of stories to tell in his broad Yorkshire accent.

One of the stories he told me was about when one of his In-laws died. He told me about the lovely mantle clock that had been promised to his wife. When her uncle passed away her brother took the clock for himself. He tried to get it working but failed, so he took it to be cleaned. Still no joy. He then took it in turn to two further experts, but each time the clock would stop working after a short interval. After a couple of years, he decided that he would give it to Jack's wife. Jack took the clock and placed it on the mantelpiece, and lo and behold, it started ticking straight away!

I had cleaned for Jack for a few years when one week I missed my cleaning day. I rang the following day only to find he had passed away. I had a good cry and then wrote the following poem for him.

Poem for a true Yorkshireman (Yorkshire dialect!)

Jack tha's a proper Yorkshire man
Yorkshire through and through,
There's many a pleasant hour I've spent
Chewin't fat wi you
Talkin about all kinds of folk
Our crazy human race
Ey lad if ony thid listened
We'd av med a better place

Al miss thi lovely Yorkshire twang,
An al miss thi wry old smile,
Al miss thi friendship that's for sure
An al miss thi unique style,
Al miss thi sound advice you gave,
And tales about thi life,
Like t'story of the haunted clock,
That ud only work for t'wife.

Al miss the times we sat an shared
Pork pies and cups of tea
Thi laugh and twinkle in your eyes
When thad teased them int bakery
We shared our sorrows and our joys,
Like only best friends do,
And tha noes my friend that though thas gon,
Al never forget you.

*A no's thas appy were thas gone
Wi't wife tha loved so dear
N soon old Sam will join you there
A noes tha wants him near
N a don't know if am going daft
But sometimes a cud swear,
That when am thinking of thee
Thas very ofen there*

The Winning Dream

I've been with my present husband now for over eight years, during which time we have had lots of adventures. We still continue to work hard with the charity, and so never have much money. One morning after we woke up Pete said to me. 'I had a really strange dream last night, I dreamt I bought two scratch cards and they were both winners'. Pete number 2, unlike Pete 1 never gambled, it did not interest him at all, but because of the dream 2 days later when we in Morrisons he disappeared off and bought two scratch cards. He came to find me in the store beaming. The first card had yielded £200 and the second another £500.

Really strange, and to his credit he has never bought a scratch card before or since.

The conclusion of this story is that it is possible to predict future events, and that they can come to us in a dream. Dreams really can come true.

My final story is an account of what happened to my daughter in law, Donna and her Mum, Angie. I thought it was such a lovely and unusual story that I should include it in my book. Angie narrated the story to me.

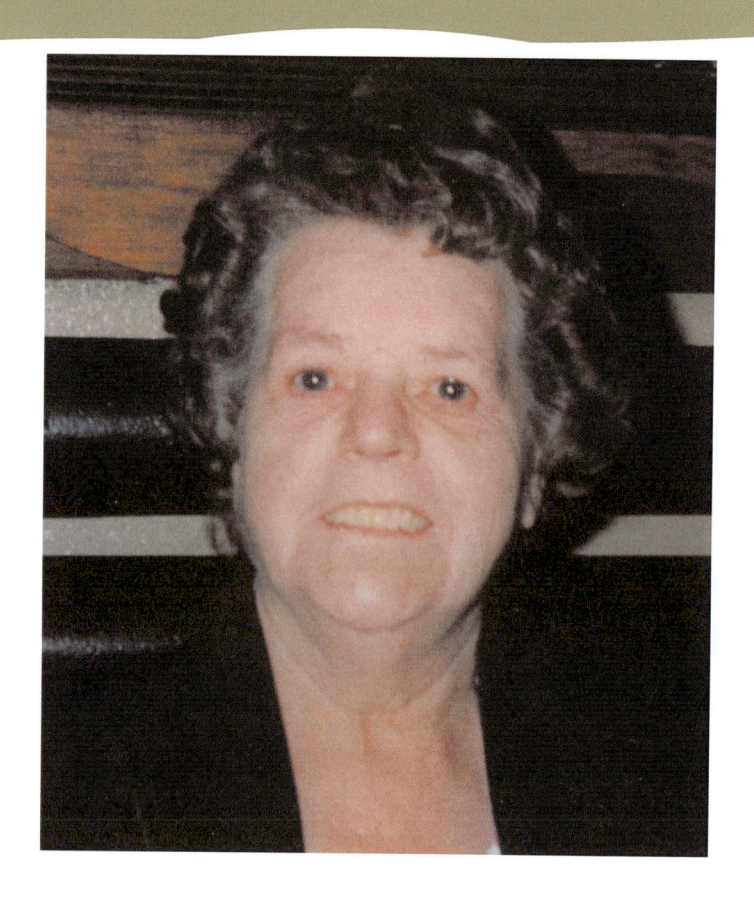

Purple Flowers

My mum's name was (and still is) Ena, short for Willamena. She was a small lady, happy outgoing and very stubborn.

She passed away in May 2010 at the age of 85 of various conditions. I was devastated.

We arranged a funeral and chose MUM in beautiful pure white flowers including roses and chrysanthemums.

A week after the funeral I went away for a week with my husband. I really needed a break, it had been a very difficult year. Whilst we were away, my daughter Donna went to visit the grave, she was very close to her Gran. She rang me in Zante and said 'you'll never guess what, Grans flowers have turned purple'. At first we thought it might be from the ribbon that was round them, but when we returned I went to visit the grave myself. The flowers were all purple, my Mums favourite colour. There was no way that it could have come from the ribbon.

On my birthday in the same year, my daughter Donna bought me some white lilies. To my amazement they slowly turned pink and then gradually purple.

Some two years afterwards, we bought a planter already planted up with flowers of every colour, which we put at the grave. The flowers gradually died off, the only one that remained living was the purple one.

My Mum loved purple, and I don't know how she did it, but I am sure it was her way of letting us know she is still around.

Celtic Benediction

Deep peace pure white of the moon to you,
Deep peace pure green of the grass to you,
Deep peace pure brown of the Earth to you
Deep peace of the sparkling dew to you
Deep peace pure blue of the sky to you.
Deep peace of the running wave to you
Deep peace of the shining stars to you
Deep peace of the Son of peace to you

Fiona Mcleod

About The Author

June started life in suburban Leeds a quiet shy girl with little self-confidence. Little did she know what a mysterious and interesting life lie ahead of her.

Her experiences during her late teens gave her a thirst to know 'The Truth' for which she drew inspiration from many sources, including her mum Joyce who was a Spiritualist and a healer, and many other magical characters that she met along life's path. She is also a mother of seven (now grown up)

She and her Zambian born friend Jennifer Musakanya co-founded a charity, which cares for and educates orphans in Mpika, Zambia. Please see www.mpika.org for details of our project.

June is now a popular and well-known member of her community in the village of Denholme, Bradford, where she runs a charity shop along with a lovely bunch of volunteers.

A percentage of the profits from this book will be donated to Mpika Village of Hope Orphanage in Zambia